WONDERS OF THE
INVISIBLE WORLD

42 Miles Press
Editor, David Dodd Lee
ISBN 978-1-7328511-3-9 (pbk. alk. paper)

Art Direction: Paul Sizer, Design: Isabelle Acosta, Production: Paul Sizer
The Design Center, Frostic School Of Art, Western Michigan University.
Printing: McNaughton & Gunn, Inc.

MILES PRESS

Indiana University South Bend Department of English

WONDERS OF THE INVISIBLE WORLD

POEMS BY CLAIRE BATEMAN

CONTENTS

Wonders are like dangers: face them, and you will pass the test.

Anthony Lane

THE NEW LONELINESS

Remember how it was before thought balloons,
a supercontinent of chaotic cognitive matter
floating just above our heads,
one huge lumpish murk?

Remember the era before alphabets were sorted,
hieroglyphics and cuneiform all jumbled together,
characters resembling machine parts
tangled with runes like forked and flaming branches?

Remember life before quotation marks,
when anything could be attributed to anyone,
so there was never a distinction
between generosity and return?

The world is tidier these days.
There's no limit to what we may accomplish
now that each of us is equipped
to take things personally.

THE VIRGIN MIRROR

After the handmaidens, blindfolded and proceeding by touch alone, have twined masses of string across its enormous silvered surface, then the mirror-keeper, also blindfolded, sets a lit match to the central knot.

When they sense that the whole skein is ablaze, they bear the burning glass to the lakeshore and lower it into the icy shallows where the mirror-keeper strikes a single blow, shattering it along every line at once.

Then they lift it in its frame to pluck out the fragments, which they swaddle individually in silk and disperse throughout the land.

Now instead of making pilgrimage in order to not look into the virgin mirror, each family can cherish a shard to not look into without ever leaving home.

ARMY OF CHILD COURIERS TRAVERSING THE PYRENEES

So light, they advance
without cracking the ice crust:

one word per mail pouch,
transparent vellum, invisible ink.

We glimpse through television snow
their narrow faces, hooded and penumbral.

They have made orphans of their mothers.
They have made mothers of us all.

MYSTIQUE ACADEMY

The first thing they taught us is that hair isn't dead. An exotic state of matter, it's composed primarily of discontinuities.

We learned that a child may become tearful or agitated on the occasion of her first hair-lengthening, and how to distract her.

We learned to identify and respond to the singular tone each follicle emits as we chanted out the strands.

We committed to memory the esoteric names of the various knots, tangles, and convolutions we'd encounter.

We were examined on the circumstances under which the separate emptiness of those knots' vital cores might, without our intervention, first stellify and then opacify into spinning inversions.

We were tested in dim rooms and assessed in harrowing glare; we were questioned underwater and evaluated in our sleep.

And don't we now tremble at our stations, wielding the sacred torches on behalf of those whose hair is finally long enough for apotheosis?

There's nothing more paradoxical than our work—red burns the slowest, then blonde, then brown.

But black goes up in a flash, as though darkness excites the flame.

PRE-HEADACHE

Hello, little pain-seed, newly lodged
behind my left eye.

Probably, even you don't know
what's next: will you break open,

send down roots, sprouting into
monstrous putrefaction,

or shrivel, shrink, dissolve,
a passing ache passingly forgotten?

After all, not everything serves
as the start of something.

Mostly, in fact, it doesn't.
Mostly, it has to be nothing,

as with the (no doubt) dozens of zealots who,
travelling the Damascus Road that particular year,

suffered a twitch, a twinge. Only Saul
was struck; the rest continued on, unchanged.

Mostly, we're all just way-stations
for migratory spasms and premonitions.

We fall with frequency and swiftness
for lovers we'll never even meet.

We sit down to pen treatises that might as well
be scrawled in disappearing ink.

Which doesn't mean, of course,
that now and then, something might not

get through: a death, a god, a love, a line or two.
So here at this point, small pain, I'll nurture you.

WEATHERS

Where I come from, everyone's helpless against the aerial onslaught of other people's mental music, those melodic fragments that run on repeat-loops through the brain.

So before we venture out on a picnic, we check the index for our chosen location, and if there hasn't been enough wind to waft away harmonic residue, we seek an alternate spot.

Before we close on a house, we scrutinize the notarized list of songs and musical passages that have accumulated there; failure to disclose even one renders a contract void.

Dating profiles feature each person's top ten, but there's no guarantee a couple's internal playlists won't evolve in opposite directions. Post-breakup, both partners still hum their ex's tunes, since music is sexually transmitted no matter how much protection lovers afflict themselves with.

A few people claim they can actually see the songs, that each possesses its own color configuration, some pale and translucent, others pulsing in primary hues; these individuals maneuver vigilantly through the streets, circumnavigating the currents, but the rest of us find ourselves continually ambushed by overlapping washes as though we're slipping between radio stations every few seconds.

It's certainly quieter in your country where those auditory echoes remain trapped inside the individual mind. Your atmosphere seems stale, almost dimensionless compared to that of my homeland, but your citizens are more volatile, reactive, prone to giving and taking offense, to aggression, litigation, every kind of strife. Such activities must serve as some kind of compensation for your predicament—with all that vacant space between you, you'll do anything to fill the air.

PENCIL SHOP

The sign by the door announces their policy: *Un crayon pour chaque mot.*

In true European style, one visits this establishment *très tôt le matin*, purchasing only what is *nécessaire pour ce jour.*

To do otherwise—to "stock up"—would this not be to prove oneself *aussi avare comme un Américain?*

Out of regard for *la situation existentielle*, there is no muzak: *with sapient et magnifique langereuse* the citizens select their blunt nouns, their slim adverbs, and *pour variété syntaxique et extension*, their stubby articles and conjunctions.

Soon, all the baskets are heaped up, weighed down, since even for *le communicateur le plus parcimonieux*, a day requires lexical abundance.

Et regarde! Par la fenêtre, le soleil se lève.

The shoppers line up to pay in priceless, inarticulate sighs.

UPKEEP

Because no one had ever paid much attention to the wall between the past and the present, it wasn't until light began to seep through that people noticed the thin spots.

Light from the past inspired acute memories: *Why, this is the radiance of my eleventh birthday morning!* someone in the present would exclaim, though later, that same person might whisper, *We stood in this noontime dazzle when we buried my sister.*

Light from the present made the citizens of the past giddy, endangering their daily routines.

As is so often the case in such situations, the administrators on both sides were split between patchers and demolitionists, the first group eager to repair and maintain, the second anxious to raze and rebuild. Various feasibility assessment projects were begun, each costly, protracted, and blundering.

Meanwhile, the wall itself became an object of fascination as everyone gathered around the weak places, the occupants of the present knocking to communicate with their ancestors, and the inhabitants of the past tapping to reach their descendants. When every attempted code turned out to be unintelligible, it was acknowledged that the longed-for newsy exchanges must be taboo, but the people refused to desist.

Eventually, they decided to preserve the wall at a precise, uniform degree of deterioration by doctoring it where it was frail enough for more than an indistinct, low-level shimmer to leak through, and tenderly scraping away at it where it was thick enough to render knocking inaudible.

This delicate engineering enterprise, colloquially known as "tuning the wall," is accomplished in both past and present by teams of trained sentinels who pace the whole length of the structure, scanning for anomalies.

Rumor has it that these sentinels have become so aware of minute structural fluctuations that they're able to evaluate the light with their eyes closed, and make their presence known to their counterparts on the opposite side without touching the surface.

So when parents behold their child rapt in the game of tiptoeing with eyes shut, hands outstretched, palms up as if braced against empty space, this is taken as nothing less than a sign of vocation, a gift from the asymptotic future.

BOOK SOUP

When the youngest child in a family feels ready to give up the self-illuminating book all little ones sleep with, it's presented at breakfast to the mother, who drops it into a large cook-pot where the night books of the older siblings have been waiting, tattered but still faithfully exuding small flashes of phosphorescence.

Everybody stands back as she pummels and kneads until the bindings come loose and the pages separate to simmer in the mingled lights all day long.

At bedtime, she ladles out a portion to each child to drink as they enter this new and longest phase of their family life, their stories glowing unseen within them.

THE DEEP CROSS-SECTIONAL PLUNGE

I keep always on my person the deed to my pinkie-ring-size plot of land, a narrow cylinder slicing through fescue and fungal soil, clots of hair and reticulations of bone, sinkholes and methane pockets, infinitesimal winged creatures soaring in soil—

yes, there is flight underground; there are crosswinds, flumes and estuaries; aquifers and cavernous suspensions; flames and bogs and tides where gravity self-deforms as though straining to flow sideways; the chalk-white roots of mountains; inverted trees with constellations of mica flakes glinting in their branches; the skeletons of miniature albino horses in migration; petrified Viking ship beams folded in with glacial leavings; radioactive isotopes; oscillating magnetic fields; solar neutrinos to which the earth is mere transparency—

all that abides below or wanders, descends, falls through to the precise midpoint of the innermost core.

I am happy, no, I am relieved to affirm that everything rising toward the opposite side is someone else's responsibility.

A DIAGRAMMED SENTENCE

is burnished in flight,
all extension and emergence,
transcending every controversy
between the functional and ornamental,
the technological and organic.
A diagrammed sentence
is sinuous and sleek,
serrated in profile,
whip-like in acceleration.

I came too near
a diagrammed sentence once.
I should have been warned
by those astringent fumes,
that aroma of asepsis.
Now I stump through the world,
testifying from within my encasing
of haemostatic gauze
that the disassembly of my flesh
was not executed in malice,
and bearing witness
to what I glimpsed up close:

something was missing,
something had broken loose
or perhaps had never been captured.

Only absence could have made
the sentence so swift
it failed to cast a shadow
or leave a wake.

THE INVISIBILITY CLOAK

According to rumor, some purchasers choose to experience invisibility only in a solitary state—before donning the cloak, they lock their doors and pull their shades.

Maybe they get some kind of psychosexual kick out of being inside of but unable to observe their own bodies, or they use invisibility as homeopathic self-treatment for existential irresolution, or the cloak functions as a *koan* by which one simultaneously is and is not present to oneself. Or maybe they so enjoy the delectable sensation of invisibility that they simply want to savor it without distraction.

But you're certain you'd never be one of them—quite the contrary, in fact; you wear the invisibility cloak only when you're around other people.

The problem, however, is that you become just as invisible to yourself as you are to everyone else; if you spill something on the fabric, you have to feel around for the stain so you can dab it with a visible detergent stick, and if the hem gets caught in a car door, you know only by the tug, the tearing sound, and the low, anguished cry of the cloak itself—inaudibility costs so much extra that hardly anyone springs for it.

And you can't glimpse your own physical boundaries, so you trip and knock things over even more frequently than you do without the cloak, though isn't that the very reason you saved up for the cloak in the first place, to escape (or at least hide) your ineptitude?

No less remarkable than invisibility itself is its failure, which gives the appearance of something appearing from nothing.

Your sister-in-law's cloak from Amazon-Used came with a mere six-hour guarantee; because she wasn't keeping close enough track to leave the party in time, it looked to everyone there as though she'd sprung into existence right in front of them.

What happens to you is only slightly less alarming: when the best-by date rolls over while you're in a darkened movie theatre, though you don't become wholly apparent, you're suddenly a kind of shimmer or blur which constitutes a disturbance, so the usher escorts you out.

What to do with an incompletely-expired invisibility cloak? You hang it in the back of your closet, but you can't stop thinking about it breathing there in the dark.

One night you slip it free from its wire, croon to it soothingly, and wrap it around you in bed as a sleeping shawl. Now you're a pioneer, the first person in history to venture into the unmapped terrain of invisible slumber!

Soon in a dream—yours or the cloak's?—you're speeding along an unfamiliar highway when what do you spot ahead of you but the mysterious, legendary mirror-plated eighteen-wheeler that haunts the nation's interstates like the Flying Dutchman.

You hit the gas, change lanes, and pull alongside it, peering through your window into the sealed cargo space with your dream-x-ray-vision to see... nothing at all!

This must be the mobile holding tank of the infamous rogue cloaks that are themselves invisible and exponentially contagious. Any contact with a human renders that person invisible forever, along with anyone that person touches and anyone the touched person touches, and so on.

The dream spooks you. Your cloak is almost out of "juice," so to speak; you can't shake the premonition that instead of properly expiring to become just an ordinary, run-of-the-mill, silk-on-silk-brocade-with-gemstone-constellations outerwear, it will turn into a rogue cloak, and then there you'll be, without any relief from invisibility—what will that do to your already defective ability to navigate the world?

And imagine the ensuing pandemic—invisible obstetrical teams attempting to facilitate the birth of invisible babies, invisible coroners trying to locate and identify the invisible dead, not to mention all the chaos between those beginning and end-of-life scenarios. Surely you owe it to society to throw the cloak into the sea where it will never again encounter a human.

So off you go toward the nearest pier.

The cloak seems to weigh more with every step you take, as though invisibility is the heaviest element in the universe or the garment is actively resisting.

Problematic as the cloak has been, and dangerous as it soon may be, you sense that you'll actually miss it—by the time you've reached the edge and are gazing down into the waves, you're feeling pre-nostalgic for the softness and sheen of the fabric, the sapphire eyes of Cygnus, the pearly strings of Lyra, and the susurrating swirl of the flame-colored inner lining.

Would it be so terrible if the whole world succumbed to the invisibility pandemic, placing all eight billion human inhabitants on equal footing as far as awkwardness is concerned?

And since it would appear as though they'd precipitously deserted the planet, with only their accoutrements and paraphernalia left behind, people would feel so disoriented that they'd tend to cluster in groups, locating each other by sound and tentative touch.

The beauty and fashion industries would unravel.

Film and television would feature hand puppets and marionettes manipulated by unseen fingers, the actors' voices the new celebrities.

On all seven continents, the spoken word would be paramount, with ever-mutating worlds of nuance to compensate for the loss of gesture and facial expression.

That's why you turn your back on the ocean and head toward the other end of the pier as you slip on the cloak or it envelops you of its own accord.

A gentle, halting, maladroit, highly verbal and intimately-bonded global population consoled primarily by puppet action—how could this be anything but an improvement?

THE LAST HUMAN BEING WHO'S NOT ON FACEBOOK

Having just broken out of rehab, you peel off the punishment mask and toss it into the river.

You wonder if your face has been altered by, or come off with, the latex.

Your court-mandated optic therapy has rendered you incapable of perceiving yourself in reflective surfaces; all you can do is run a finger over the phantom landscape of your nose and cheekbones, straining to construct a mental map of your features from minute barometric fluctuations across your real or remembered skin as the world flows around you, but the picture won't coalesce.

Perhaps your absence serves as Facebook's icy singularity, the closest it can come to anything like sensation.

Now everyone who glimpses you will shrink away in disgust at their own deviant desire to experience themselves only from the inside-out.

And the punishment mask? With luck, it'll find its way out to sea and be ingested by the Great Barrier Reef.

GROUNDED

Neither pulverized nor laid to rest in a graveyard,
the phone booths were loaded onto container ships,
then consigned to the ocean floor,
along with their superheroes
in various stages of undress,
who, weary of perusing
pulpy directories and obsolete graffiti,
now peer through glass at clouds of kelp,
awaiting a slow-motion emergency.

LOSING YOUR PHONE IS WORSE THAN LOSING YOUR SOUL BECAUSE AT LEAST IF YOU HAVE YOUR PHONE, YOU CAN TEXT YOUR SOUL

Where are you? you tap with your ever-aching thumbs,
what are you seeking?

...RUINATION, your soul replies, APOCALYPSE,
THE UPRISING OF WATER
AND THE DOWNPOURING OF FLAME!

But it doesn't work in reverse—
you can't contact your phone with your soul;
you have to venture out and hunt it down.

And when, after the requisite ordeals,
you've tenderly extracted it
from its hiding place in the Marianas Trench,
the molten gut of Mauna Loa,

or worse, that narrow space between
the driver's seat and the console
of your most recent rental car
which generates all the lostness in the universe,

and you've ritually purified it with a sterile wipe,
and charged it,
your frenzy of separation anxiety abating
as the screen starts to glow,

you decide, *This can't happen again,*
so you start to consider options,
remembering how your neighbor's brother's sys-admin
spoke freely at a barbecue last spring
about having had The Work done,
though she wouldn't say where on her body
the skin-graft phone-pouch is located,

a modification more intimate
than the most esoteric of tattoos,

and it's not as though you could guess
by looking at her, decked out as she was
in that voluminous garb

which, you suddenly realize,
everyone but you is sporting now,
hands moving faster than you can track
in and out of intricate openings and folds,

retrieving their phones, then returning them
only to slip them out again
at the next ding, ring, or chime,
happy marsupials of the new world.

PRINT

To qualify for the work we used to do, you couldn't be squeamish about hurrying to a death site, taking the deceased's hand in your own, and guiding their thumb to their cell phone's home-button in order to activate One-Touch ID so the people on their contacts list could be notified. We were famous for our steadiness in even the most grisly of circumstances, and everyone honored us, since all would eventually require our services, as it's a felony for any mere civilian to engage in even indirect contact with someone else's phone, their external soul.

But ours is now a vanished vocation, for almost every citizen carries on their person a pocket-size glass screw-top jar containing a wax replica of their own thumb. Heart attack, suicide, car wreck? No matter the cause of death, this little look-alike is ready, the swirl at the fleshy tip pre-engraved by accu-laser to duplicate that of the owner.

In fact, it's typical to become so emotionally attached to the proxy thumb that it remains with its owner's body in the final state of rest. Some people stipulate that it be placed in their pocket, others in their hand, still others right against the heart. And since most of them want funeral garb designed for their digits, specialty miniature tailor shops have sprung up everywhere, their neon thumb-signs flashing. Often, the attire reveals how the owner envisions their deepest self—the most stolid of civil servants may array her thumb in a matador's cape, for instance, while a champion wrestler may outfit his thumb in a postal worker's uniform.

Of course, we can't speculate about whether the dead miss the human touch, our hands tenderly uniting them with their phones for the final impression, but we know the nostalgia we suffer for the thrill of the dispatcher's message, the rush to the location, the moment when our grasp became a temporary tabernacle for that small, nearly weightless emblem of singularity.

GRIP

Sometimes it's nearly impossible
to sketch to the paper's edge;
the lines force their way inward,
compelled toward the center.

To break that field's hold,
you may poke holes
in the vellum using
a small device designed
for that purpose:

the gravity-defying,
line-releasing awl
with its delicate biomorphic prongs
which retract a nanosecond
after puncturing the surface
so as to not mar the next sheet,

and then release
a film of sealant
that hides but does not
saturate the wounds.

Now you can range;
now you can adorn,
rearrange, and ply
your space. Now
you can rampage.

OUTSKIRTS

It is good to dwell
on the sky's shore
where you work the horizon,
soothing it with salves,
smoothing it with pumice
in spots where it
tends to splinter.

But each time
the summons arrives,
no less distinct
for the distance
it had to travel,
you turn as you always do
in obligatory self-gathering,

and off you set,
on your two flesh feet,
with all that way in the way
between you and the far-flung interior,

since no matter the occasion,
everyone deems it
your duty
to come to *them*.

A BEDTIME STORY

Once there was a country whose people accrued an enormous collective sleep deficit because they were always at work, enduring perpetual bleariness to keep productivity high.

But when their fatigue finally became so irresistible they would occasionally find themselves starting to drift off toward the clouds, it became clear to the Committee in Charge of Emergencies that something had to be done.

And so a retrieval team trekked to the Storehouse of Sleep and braved its darkness only to find that the great drifts and mounds of unused slumber were not only rotting but had metamorphosed into tiny translucent worms.

In the face of this disaster, what could the travelers do but scoop up samples of these creatures and carry them home to be placed in a viewing tank?

The citizens, all hanging onto each other in case of sudden buoyancy, waited in line for a glimpse.

Alas, our sleep, our poor lost sleep, everyone sobbed as the worms shriveled as though ready to die.

But after a brief season of this apparent desiccation, the specimens began sprouting thread-like tendrils or filaments, also translucent, which grew swiftly until the tank was webbed with this substance that could not be identified as vegetable, animal, or mineral.

Now the people began to be afraid; no one truly understands the nature of sleep, and this mutation that had sprung from it (comprised of all their undreamt nightmares, perhaps, or some strain of polysomnia or retrosomnia?) seemed even more mysterious. And what if it were to break through the glass to release toxins or smother the population?

After agitated deliberations, the Committee in Charge of Emergencies decided that the substance would have to be destroyed while still in this nascent phase.

It fell to the fire-fighters to unseal the lid and reach in, no doubt because of their enviable, state-of-the-art protective gloves.

The webbing itself was so silky they could scarcely hold onto it, but as it slipped from their fingers, instead of wafting off into the breeze, it plunged to the ground, emitting an eerie keening sound and attempting to burrow into the soil, for it experienced this alien realm of direct light and oxygen as a kind of torment.

The crowd took a few steps back, horrified, but the head of the Committee cried out in jubilation: suddenly, he had a plan.

Now the sleep-webs are cultivated, harvested, and processed so that clumps of it can be stitched into fabric casings which are then attached to the citizens' shoulders.

Ceaselessly questing downward, the web-stuff counteracts the anti-gravitational effects of chronic exhaustion.

Its uncanny lamentation continually fills the air, but nobody minds, since any noise one hears without respite soon becomes, for all practical purposes, inaudible.

Thus, everyone remains both permanently awake and successfully terrestrial, maintaining quotas.

Wings to keep people on the ground! See how even the most intractable problems contain their own solutions?

INFANT PHOTO

One's birthday suit was
all compact back then,
unseasoned little sac darkening
in Kodak bathwater.

The ancients believed
objects continuously emit
images of themselves like
ephemeral, molting skins
that fly through the air
to be optically absorbed.

What could be
at the core?

More.

MEN AS TREES, WALKING

There they go, everywhere you look,
with their stumpy gait—

slippage of shadow, roughness of shank,
all knuckly protuberance and scraggy skin,

like those noble hardwoods of childhood
that loosened their roots at midnight
to wander as they would.

By dawn, each was settled at its post,
all those churned-up wakes
healing over.

SPEAK

After the last remaining waterfall had thawed in winter, unweaving the warp and weft of its silence; after people no longer gathered as by a hearth to watch the shreds of the only surviving glacier emit its ancient kinetic blue; after the waters had risen and everyone had taken refuge on rafts of all kinds and sizes lashed together, there came a generation of children who'd never set foot on soil, yet cried out in their play, "Look, I'm a tree, I'm a horse, I'm a mountain, I'm the *ground*!" not fully comprehending these words, so that sometimes trees poured themselves out in avalanche, and sometimes the ground pranced on its hind legs—yes, there were horses rising up to offer shade and fruit, there were mountains galloping long, bearing riders, though these diversions were awkward, not from this lexical confusion, but from the bulky protective garb no one was tempted to remove since they'd witnessed the work of sunlight on carelessly uncovered skin; they'd heard those sounds extracted from the body as though flesh at this point in history had finally found its voice.

LUX AETERNA

According to rumor, true night is not, in fact, extinct; the very last bead of it nestles under glass in a government vault, translucent and darkly shining, like a phantom pearl to be rolled between the fingers, slipped under the tongue.

This is merely a fable, of course, yet isn't the notion of theft worth lingering on?—or kidnapping—as if anyone could set that ransom.

Who but a saint or hero would break it open to unfurl as weather into which we all might step, abandoning the dusk-emitting lanterns contrived by our industrious engineers?

RISING TIME

One afternoon, three children playing in a back corner of their garden came upon a pair of large stone fingertips sticking up out of the soil, pressed closely together as though the hands were positioned palm to palm.

Of course, they wanted to uncover him, so they immediately set to work, the eldest with his sterling silver baby spoon; the middle child with her sea-shell-shaped sugar spoon; and the youngest with a runcible spoon.

They dug for a while, and then they took off their sweaters and dug some more, the gap around the fingertips growing as the wrists became visible. The hands were shiny, almost translucent, with cloudy brownish knots and veins.

I wonder how far down he goes, said the youngest.

The middle child said, *If there's a whole stone body, this will take a very long time, especially if he's as tall as he surely must be!*

The eldest child said, *We'll dig for a year if we must.*

By almost sundown, they'd gotten to just below the elbows, which were not bent, but straight.

While the children ate their dinner, they speculated about this. Was the man praying or diving, or, in this particular case, were praying and diving the same thing?

Still, said the middle child, *it must be an awkward position to hold for a long time. Try it.*

Right there at the table, all three of them stretched their arms and hands into the same position, and it was indeed uncomfortable.

At this point, the mother came in with pie, bubbly baked apple oozing fragrantly out of the crust.

Whatever are you doing? she asked.

They told her about the giant.

My goodness, she exclaimed. *Is it that time already?*

What time? asked all three of the children at once.

Rising Time, said the mother, and went to the telephone, removing her apron as she always did, though of course, no one she called could see her.

She dialed a few numbers, spoke quietly.

When the father came in from the train, she greeted him as always, and then said, *We must have our dinner early tonight, as soon as the children have cleared their plates. It's Rising Time.*

Already? said the father. *Things do move along in this world, don't they, whether you're thinking about them or not. Well, I'll prepare the luminaries while you wash up.*

And he went to put his hat and coat in the hall closet.

Mother! said the children, nearly all at once. *What's Rising Time?*

She frowned at them. *You don't know?* she asked.

They declared vehemently that they didn't.

You're teasing me, aren't you?

They declared even more vehemently that they were serious.

I thought your father had explained it to you, she said.

No!

The father came back in. *What's this hubbub?*

The children claim that you never told them about Rising Time, the mother said.

I assumed you did, said the father.

Both parents were visibly chagrined

Well, said the mother. *We did teach them about table manners—*

*—and strangers—*added the father.

—and how to safely cross the street, said the mother.

—and how to save their pennies, said the father.

—and how to say please, thank you, and excusez-moi at the appropriate times, said the mother, *so I suppose we can't be considered altogether negligent. Nevertheless, we should have told them.*

Yes, said the father. *It's a shame that we let it slip. Of course, we can't get into it now.*

No, said the mother. *We must get on with things.*

And so they did.

In less than an hour they were gathered in the back garden, which adjoined the neighbors' back gardens.

All the parents had brought out odd blown-glass balloon lamps lit from within by, as the father called them, "non-oxygenated candles," and everyone, including the grown-ups, had found their digging spoons, though the few people who used them seemed merely to be loosening the dirt from around the edges of the holes, for now in every garden, giant stone people with pressed-together hands were emerging from the earth on their own.

Indeed, the children's giant had come up several inches during dinner, so more could be seen of him than of the other giants, which made the children feel a bit better about the fact that some gardens boasted entire stone families whereas they themselves had only the one fellow.

It was like any other village occasion—the grown-ups chatted in small clusters as the very young children slept on their shoulders or played around their feet, and some of the older ones perched in the lower branches of trees while others looked on or chased each other until they finally curled up to doze on the benches.

And as the stars crept across the sky, the earth continued both to rotate and revolve, and countless waves hurled themselves against countless shores with only a few individuals taking any notice at all of this vast, continual effort, the stone people worked their way up.

Finally, a little before dawn, the parents gathered the children.

The giants had completed their surfacing and were now fully visible in their heavy brogues and their soil-and-leaf-encrusted garments with stone wrinkles and folds.

Their faces and hands were slightly bluish in the echoey non-oxygenated light, as if they might be chilly without the earth around them, and their stone thoughts were impossible to guess.

Everyone gazed at them in silence.

Then the fathers snipped the strings and released the luminaries into the air.

With them rose the giants, the children's giant a little ahead of the rest as though he was their leader or perhaps a scout.

Up and up they went, ever smaller as they plumbed the darkness.

The parents blinked and rubbed their necks and passed around glasses of glittering champagne.

And from the same wooden boxes in which the glass lamps had rested, they lifted fist-sized, exceedingly dense stone eggs which they allowed the children to touch and wonder at for a few moments before they dropped them into the holes where the giants had been, sprinkled them with ordinary sugar, and covered them with the earth that had been displaced by the giants' self-excavation.

Then it was time to collect the scarcely-used digging spoons, the flesh-and-blood babies and children, and the fluted champagne glasses, and go inside for breakfast, since things do move along in this world, whether you're thinking about them or not.

THE LIMITED NUMBER OF ITEMS THE MIND CAN HOLD

A list is a sieve composed of exclusions.

The idea of enumeration is essential to the list, as are alphabetical order, entropy, and the small infinities between items.

If you were to write your list on a flat rubber ball and then pump it up, the items would flee from each other along with everything in the expanding universe.

Only God experiences each entity as its own category, knowing infinite lists of one. This is why it's difficult for us to bless everything at once, so perhaps it's best to simply recite the alphabets of all nations.

At this point in the millennium, humanity's two favorite lists are the list of what could have been otherwise and the master list of errors, which is sheerly theoretical, though we embellish its margins with biomorphic botanicals.

But the errors don't want to be tallied on paper; they want to reunite in the world as one enormous Ur-substance, a Pangaea of wrongness, and while it would be noble to assist them, and we find it appealing, the idea of having them all conveniently in one place, this is a task that remains high on our list of things that aren't on our list of things to do.

SHIFTING

The peasant begs the hermit
to come to his dying wife, leads him

to a shelter of brambles where a wolf bitch
wallows in her own blood.

Don't be afraid—doesn't it always
start that way?—*to bless me.*

A woman's voice; he can tell by the vowels
which pocket of the county she was raised in.

Later, he won't remember
whether she went as woman, wolf,

or neither, shifting.
He'll hold in his mind

three pictures of her,
each necessary, complete:

crown of the head where hair whorls,
span of wrist, foreshortened,

these things happening
less frequently now—

insinuation of road into woodland,
and all day long the axes ringing.

He's heard rumors, a doctor
who buys gallows-corpses,

lays them out between candles
and rows of knives,

placing the extracted organs
in clean bowls for study.

Deep in his forest
the hermit feels the heartbeat

double, slow, and cease.
He strokes the coarse hair,

gazes into the two gold eyes,
and closes them.

INVENTORY

So they decided to attire the ocean, not out of any sense of prudery, but because they'd long ago appareled the cities with their hanging gardens as well as the mountains and plains; experts were reportedly drawing up projections regarding the moon and other celestial bodies in anticipation of an aeronautical future.

Also, everyone felt that the ocean resembled an enormous eye never allowed to close; after all it had done for them, didn't it deserve some respite?

They chose silk lined with crepe-de-chine and organza in eggshell, platinum, swan, fleece, snow, chalk, and pearl—a masterwork of exquisite understatement—and laid it out upon the waters like the long-lost white map of foldable space.

Released from the work of glaring at its nemesis the sky, the ocean asked itself, *What am I inside this gown?*

Though new to soul-searching, the ocean intuited that nothing could be learned in an overwrought condition, so it labored to make itself still as possible despite having long ago become habituated to its own agitation.

Yet gradually, over centuries, the tides and currents released their tension and embraced each other horizontally while the waves flattened themselves into a slow float.

As the ocean began to palpate its plants and creatures, its embedded caverns and mountain ranges, its running crevices and iterative turns, it was darkly revealed to itself as the lapidary marvel it had always been.

I *am voltaic blue*, it murmured; I *am incarnadine gold, diaphanous green.*

Meanwhile, on land, the other coverings gradually frayed, unraveled, disintegrated, and were dispersed on the wind.

Since nudity of all kinds was coming back into vogue, no one replaced them.

.

Only the ocean's garb remained, though after so many generations, the people couldn't imagine that there was anything other than some kind of wasteland beneath—they'd forgotten all about the great waters

Eventually, in keeping with the new aesthetic honoring exposure, they decided to take off the covering.

The removal crew went down to the shoreline with long hooks and pulled back the silk, rolling it up on the beach like a giant scroll.

There it was: the briny deep.

It's a beast! A monster! some shouted, and indeed, it did seem to writhe and slaver.

It's the underworld risen! cried others, and indeed, it did seem to exude a peculiar light.

The rest of the people said nothing, but only gazed, until one worker, near enough to be splashed, said, *No, it's just water.*

The freshly disclosed ocean found itself surprised to be in happy colloquy with the sky as waves and clouds wondered together, *Are we depth all the way up or surface all the way down?* The people, however, were so startled that it didn't occur to them to wax philosophical; neither did they ponder such questions later, as they were busy re-inventing ships, navigation, and equipment with which to excavate sunken treasure.

As for the white fabric, it turned out to be too finely stitched to disintegrate and too vast and bulky to burn. It occupied miles and miles of beach, calling into question the new hypothesis that the amount of nakedness in the world was a supreme constant which could be reconfigured and reapportioned but never expanded or diminished.

HEAT

Yes, we're sisters still, though not like when we shared a single pair of swansdown slippers; two of us would huddle barefoot by the hearth guarding the cold cord-wood so the third could venture out to hunt for flame.

But because the world is full of oblique inflorescences, unlikely correspondences, and things disguised as or inextricable from other things, often, the seeker would bring home not fire but a wriggling of fox kits; a bewilderment of bees; a ladle spilling molten butter.

Yet now we find ourselves chillier in prosperity than during that night we spent trying to thaw our hands in the light of the blooming forsythia the shod sister must have braved piercing distances to find.

FATHOM

Of drowning in the sky there can be no end.
Even the sky drowns in place,
plummeting, shocked to be vertical,
and only as it gaspingly approaches the ground
does it start to perceive its transparent nature—
all along, it had assumed its work was occlusive,
but now it's exposed as tender,
woundable, light and slow.
And where did anyone learn such drowning
if not from looking up, only to stumble,
knocked off-balance, filling with sky
as it continuously arrives for the first time?

The point where the sky is most accessible is the sky itself.
The point where the sky is least comprehensible is also the sky,
hosting migratory trenches, abysses, ridges and ranges of air,
shifting between stillness and seismic tremor—
calamity-sapphire, blown-crystal black,
aquamarine with dollops of mauve and rose,
or milky with held-back snow, amplifying silence.

There's currently no clinical protocol
for individuals who trudge through the world
heads down, sky-rejecting, gravity-obsessed.
Various treatments have been attempted—
ultrashortwave diathermy and radiosurgery
as well as elliptical back-of-the-neck tapping with ice wands;
musical castigations and interrogations;
and repeated backwalking through mirrors
according to the theory that the sky *began* as a mirror,
that is, an attenuated reflective amalgam
of water and ante-historical liquid glass
whose mutated off-castings still emerge
now and then from Saharan sands.

Older, long-abandoned speculations include
sky as ultra-luminous rarified wax
exuded by bees vibrating faster than the speed of light;
sky as an ethereal pearl still forming in layers
around some ancient galactic irritation;
and sky as resonance filling a concave hollow earth
whose inner shell we inhabit, enlivened
by the central electromagnetic blaze that is the sun.

But regarding this tragic phenomenon of sky-refusal—
in the continued absence of a cure,
mothers are taking the matter into their own hands,
tossing their infants into the air every morning
to gulp clear tropospheric bubbles that expand
as the child grows here in the elapsing present
where every full-capacity human
measures larger on the inside
than bodily parameters should allow,
maintaining that paradoxical volume
until the final breath when sky reunites with sky
as fresh self-drowning, since for this voluminous
transposition, the way out is the way in.

AESOP'S GOOSE LAMENTS

First the low, familiar ache,
then the heaviness, slick rush and slide,
and there in the straw it glows
heart-warm, egg of sheerest gold,
solid all through, or hinged
with a diamond window shielding
the Nativity, each wise man's face
furrows of sculpted grief,
or with a tiny hole
through which to contemplate
the earth inaccessible in sculpted jade,
mountain contour and mother-of-pearl sea.

He thinks I do it on purpose.
Everything he does, he does on purpose.
He makes his knife sing
on the whetstone until it's nothing
but heat and obedience.

HABITAT

Though no doubt she can sense our presence, the solitary gown doesn't startle. Stitched of taffeta and crinoline, with pearl buttons down the back under the pinned-on veil, and six hoop petticoats to buttress her, she holds her ground atop a craze of asphalt crack lines sprouting chicory, mustard grass, and thistle.

In the dusk, she looks as though she could generate her own microclimate—a swirl of snowflakes, perhaps, even in this unseasonable heat—surely the neighborhood could use a tender, feathery mantle of white; the pavement's pitted and churned, hyenas lope across formerly fastidious lawns, and wild pigs forage in rose gardens overrun by scrub.

Feral yet unafraid, she must have wandered away from her pack, though she won't be alone for long; the others can't be far off, and they move swiftly, not only when they're hunting, but just as often for the sheer sensation of wind through gauze. From the air they'd look like spun sugar dollhouse dresses (if planes were still flying), but here on the ground their elegance is inextricable from their ferocity.

According to legend, it's lucky to catch a glimpse of them at full speed, but whether or not that's true, it does fill the heart with joy to behold them in the wild after that long era they spent asphyxiating in wardrobes or pining behind plate glass.

SCATTER

And here we see where the pages of the ocean
were torn from their logbook as if in meticulous rage,
though there's no debris adhering to the binding,
as might so easily have been the case.
What to do with this stiff and empty cover?
Pack it with snow and staple it all around,
so it can retain its shape until the committee
rends it open and shakes it out face-down,
inviting the ragged pages to return
in just the right sequence
from every place they've flown.

THE ROOM MOTHER'S TALE

In my time, I've fostered
many rooms, each
from its nest extracted,
trucked to heartland
where some hollow structure
had been languishing.

They say once hatched,
a room grows quickly,
fills to the brim with
fittings, fixtures, artifacts.

"Life" happens there,
or so I'm told—to me,
this notion must remain
abstract, a bubble-womb,
remote, intact.

WE HADN'T EXPECTED HUMMINGBIRDS IN PURGATORY,

let alone enough sweetness to attract them,
as well as honeybees the size of infants' fists
hanging upside down in anther all morning
and drowsing in peonies through the night.
We hadn't known there would be
star-shaped holes and hole-shaped stars,
time-lapse visitations of oak and elm,
their shadows like nets let down from the branches,
rush and influx of wind like floods
through roots upwelling.

Every dawn after we drink from the river
that alternates between blue and black
except for when it's white or transparent,
we must map something fresh to unknow:
the exquisite, the intricate, the unsufferable—
all separated by what connects them
and vice versa—you'd think by now
they'd have canceled each other out.

By some historical damage or design,
our map hosts an aperture the size of a human eye
that never appears in the same place twice.
Often we find ourselves crowding around it
as though it's a little window.
What do we hope to discover,
someone gazing back from the other side?
There is no other side.

LITTLE DISAPPOINTMENT SONGS

The Famine Candle

Cracked open, the candle looks like
cake inside, but it persists as paraffin
though you can't stop breaking and tasting,
tasting and breaking.

Invisible Tattoos Everywhere

Do fugitive images navigate through zones
of dermis and tendon to hide themselves in bone,
or does marrow so crave inscription that it drinks
ink like elixir, leaving the surface blank?

Not Having Your Cake, Not Eating It Either

No flour no sugar no egg no cream
no swelling no rising no wick no flame
no repose in the light of a tiered incandescence
no glycerin surge in the blood and brain.

Angel with Flaming Sword

There's a parallel text
into which you may never look:
*The Book of Who You Were
When You Read the Book.*

THE THING ABOUT THE MAIL

The thing about the mail is that much of it's invisible *en route*. You hand over your envelope or package to the carrier, and then watch it disappear, first gradually from the corners, then faster and faster until the center winks out. In this it's so much like the problem of prayer that carriers are regarded as a subset of the priestly class, for they traffic in spectral exchanges. (To gain employment at the postal service, you must first prove that you're a mnemonic savant, able to hold each address in memory after having seen it only once, and to recognize each item by its heft and feel in your hands.)

Sadly, however, the only mail that never achieves invisibility status is junk mail, which remains not only hyper-present but indestructible by immolation, immersion, shredding. When buried or drowned, it indefatigably rises; when placed between scissors, it becomes so slippery it prevents the blades from meeting; and when consigned to flames, it won't even smolder.

Everyone loves to watch mail reappear in the recipient's grasp, except for the bills, of course.

*

No, the thing about the mail is that it can't decide what story it adds up to. It used to think that it was the innocence-to-experience story, but now it wonders if it's the interrogative/imperative story, the talismanic/oracular story, or even the epiphanic story. It ponders the troubling phenomenon of consciousness in the universe; it contemplates the question of origins.

But when it sleeps, it dreams that it's none of these stories—that it is, in fact, merely decoy mail sent out to draw off the gobblers who hunt in packs to devour unread correspondence.

*

No, the thing about the mail is that a letter sent out whole arrives in pieces over the span of a generation—a word here, a sprinkling of punctuation marks there—and must be painstakingly reassembled with no assurance of accuracy, like a symphony whose every note and rest has been packed separately in a small black lacquered box, all of the boxes hidden throughout a forest amidst the underbrush and among the branches and in the crowns and cavities of trees so that those who find them have to string them on the staff according to their collective best guess.

*

No, the thing about the mail is that separately and in small bundles, each item is peaceable, inert, but at a certain level of accumulation they begin to fight and cannibalize each other.

Sometimes, as one would expect, it's the ponderous package or the oversize envelope bulky with tax documents that proves to be the alpha, but just as often, it's the simple photocopied flyer-with-a-stamp or the reticent little "save the date" notice that comes out intact, while all that's left of the rest is a bit of fine gray powder—a mixture of white space and ink—that swiftly dissipates into the atmosphere.

Most postal workers shudder at the forbidden practice of baiting and tormenting individual mail items to intensify their aggression, but there are always those few who abuse their official trust and set up fight rings, placing bets on which items will attain dominance.

*

No, the thing about the mail is that it suffers air, it suffers light, it suffers touch by human hands and the walls of various conduits and receptacles. Mail is made of thought and feeling, cognition and sensation, and thus feels at home only inside the cranial cavity, the chambered heart; none of these things belongs in the external world, so what mail desires is for time itself to slip its gears and run in reverse, the signature disappearing first as the letters of the signer's name evaporate, then, with its varying degrees of nearness or distance, the complimentary close—eternally yours, hugs and kisses, love, cordially, sincerely, all best, regards—or the admonition—be good, stay safe, keep the faith, write soon, send money please—then the body of the missive, bottom to top—gossip, chitchat, argument, declaration, apology, explanation, invitation, and at last, the salutation as the paper goes blank, while within its author, the communicative impulse begins to dissolve until all that's left is grievance, remorse, or desire in a pure pre-linguistic state.

*

Yes, the thing about the mail is that it's with us no longer. Walking down a street where any mailboxes still stand, children tug on their parents' coats and ask, "What are those funny little houses on sticks?" Instead, we now live among multitudes of tiny, floating sparks that deliver information directly to the brain by entering through our eyes. Though we mostly approve of our transition from the physicality of letters to this evanescent, ubiquitous twinkling, we don't leave the mail unmemorialized; everyone takes their designated turn to don the ceremonial mourning robes of painstakingly stitched white paper and trudge the old postal routes chanting the zip codes, each number a distinct sacred tone. When a mourner goes by, you must pause, incline your head, and perform the ritual gestures of indirection to honor the Two Lost Things, absence and darkness. Then you may proceed again, wending your way between the sparks.

THE PERFORATING SPIDER

To what degree we should fear her we can't know, but we extol her labor which is eleventy-seven percent more exacting than that of her arthropod relatives since she has thirteen feet—if you look closely, you might glimpse the flickering of their stochastic puncture-patterns on the moving spider map of the universe known also as the interdimensional network of negative space.

Nor can we discern whether she achieved her position or it was primordially imposed on her—is she an angel, perhaps a lesser god?

We do know that these feet are named respectively 1 absence 2 anomaly 3 discontinuity 4 the specious present 5 ellipsis 6 antithesis 7 stealth 8 the fugue-state 9 the lost sea 10 the anti-tonic 11 the oblique gravitational force 12 polysemy 13 cipher. Note also her wing-buds, infolded, either prophecy or vestigial legacy of aerial predation.

Of course, she must be infinitesimal to cover so much territory all at once; thanks to her choreographic exploits, we don't have to suffer a world devoid of gaps, fissures, micro-spaces in which to turn, then turn again.

Where would we be without the stutter in the testimony, the digital glitch, the snapped string in the middle measure as the dancers pause to reconsider their partner choice?

And consider the sun, our sole domestic hearth in the sidereal universe—without the perforating spider's footwork there'd be no absence in its core for hydrogen atoms to flow into toward fusion, no coronal holes forming and reforming for solar particles to slip through.

Even more locally, consider hair—without her, each of our heads would be burdened by a single solid clump non-navigable by breeze or comb or reconnoitering fingers—no strands, no braids, no weaves, no waves, in just the same way as thought in the brain would seize, a frozen mass without interstices for passage and transformation.

Prior to her: that Ur-time when music constituted one indigestible monster entity. Then in she stepped, and up sprang the rests, the intervals, so each note could recognize itself as itself, discrete.

Thus we count on her for hesitation, indecision, the lapse where intention slackens and the soul quakes because eventually, everything that can happen will happen, though not necessarily to you.

Were we to beg her for advice on how to bear the sensation of existence (so massive and bursting, so delicate and light), if she cared to reply (which she decidedly would not), she'd advise us in her arcane alphabet comprised of nothing but holes—like a kind of inverse Braille—to move even deeper into the configuring darkness, the constellary wound where it's always indigo o'clock, history o'clock, collapse o'clock. If we didn't live here, we'd undoubtedly long for it.

THE ORDINARY COURSE OF THINGS: A CENTO

1.

All streams flow into the sea,
yet the sea, that spacious wound,
is never full,

just as thirst rarely answers
the simplest star: blue flame
projecting distance, a bell
of darkness, known.

How small the creation!
Hurried through many changes naked,
finally compelled to crawl,
it does not wake,

I wish—I cannot think—
a sort of vague feeling comes over me,
glimpse of lamp burning low—
that I have asked all this before.

2.

The mind is its own place,
a far-off hazy multitudinous assemblage
of bells, and wheels, and flowers
at a high pitch of velocity;
little craters all burning, lava flowing uphill;
gigantic ruins and the strange bright constellations;
shadows of clouds feeding on each other—
a moving curtain of the earth and sky
that has been already in the ages before us—
Was it person? Was it thing?
was it touch or whispering?

It comes without meaning
a knot on a piece of string,
minute in its distinctness,
as it threads the darkness.

3.

When thunder and lightning were first found
to be due to secondary causes,
some regretted to give up the idea
that each flash was caused by
the direct hand of God,
their regal gold-inwoven tatters,
the shadow passed from between us
through the dark Areal Hall,
a double consciousness,
that crooked tree, its roots full of caves
that had grown as the world grew
in the changing light of heaven and of eyes.
Let it glide where it will,
like wings of flaws and holes:
time will do wonders.

Note: Comprised of words and phrases found in writings by Charles Darwin and
George Eliot as well as from the book of Ecclesiastes, *Paradise Lost*, and Charles Kingsley's
The Water Babies.

ABUNDANCE

I want to live in Kmart,
slit from slick plastic
the winter comforters,
pile them thickly high,
and then ascend,
a story princess
beneath the apogee reclining,
there to place in dazzling array
cheap incandescent stars—
O canopy of my desiring—
in Kmart, all alone.

When I was beautiful,
the aisles did make way
for my long legs
and redgold hair,
a burnished galleon
flying through,
sails taut, pennants aflutter,
though none of this
did I with accuracy know,
believing the shapes
and patterns of the world
to be simply so.

But now in every
shopper wheeling by,
a human soul shrinks
from my cloudy eye,
stitched lip,
and bulging chin,
the functional shoulder
torturously higher.

Once, I heard
a Kmart mother
remark in passing

to her sister:
If my second baby
had been my first,
There wouldn't have
been another
a statement
I most seriously
ponder:

would I feel
better or worse
if this second life
had been my first,
an *only*?

Now when I dream about
that redgold womanchild
in gleaming spandex
gliding up the aisle,

my mouth twists
into something
not unlike a smile

because she is
so frightened to see
through mazes of abundance
appearing:
me

though all I wish to do
is wrap my crooked arm

warily
around her.

METAPHORICALLY SPEAKING

A fluency of bathwater with a fleet, a flurry, an extravagance of babies ricocheting off each other like pool balls run amok: babies bald or fully-fluffed or with downy eaglet hair. The babies are dense and compact, the bathwater's frothy; the babies are uncouth, the bathwater's refined with fragrant spices wasted on the babies, and lily pads bearing jeweled frogs whose emerald-studded hides the babies long to gum, but the frogs are ever escaping while the babies' mouths itch and burn, so what's their only option for relief? It's certainly the soap, that lonesome bar bobbing in the suds with ridges to prove it's already been tried and rejected, forgotten, sighted and gripped, bitten then dropped anew in an orgy of intermittent object retention as babies and bathwater bubble and bloom together, the babies steeping like plump little teabags, their fingers wrinkled, their toes wrinkled, even their belly buttons wrinkled, both innies and outies, for the babies were born drown-proof; they got buoyancy for their superpower as they came up through the drain in reverse-whirlpools piped in from some foamy subterranean wonderland, but somewhere amidst the mess, the mass, the mightily whipped-up mousse of froth and motion, in the eldest of babies something is breaking through: a bud—a milk tooth—a single incisor, the first of their classic labors in the world.

THE PRISONERS

Each is chained to a post an arm's length from her bed so that she can inhale the scent of the pillow and suffer the pull of the mattress' gravity, though she's forever unable to approach.

And they're not allowed to mourn their slumber.

Failure to comply is immediately detected by The Apparatus, calibrated to set off alarms in the presence of even the most muted tinge of grief-for-sleep.

The Apparatus is so specific in its grief-for-sleep sensitivity that possibly the prisoners have learned to hide their grief in other kinds of sadness The Apparatus isn't primed to notice.

This is one theory about why they're still standing after all these years.

Another theory is that they abandoned their bodies immediately before they were taken into custody, and their souls passed into neighboring dormancies—the staticky sleep of house crickets, the one-lane sleep of road trance, the cartilaginous sleep of stingrays, the monochrome sleep of ghosts.

And yet a third theory is that though the arrests occurred without warning, they were far from unexpected—that there had, in fact, been significant preparation, not only by the prisoners but by their mothers and grandmothers all the way back through eleven generations of clandestine incremental bed-ingestion rituals as they practiced on pillow cases and dust ruffles, and worked their way through box springs, canopies, and headboards, incorporating the sleep residue in those structures so fully into their actual flesh that as far as The Apparatus is concerned, it doesn't even register.

THREE CENTOS

Star Head

Look directly into the face.

Radiating in a wheel-like fashion,
the absent center
(that small, wind-bearing organ)

may be removed
so that the entire corolla
breaks open.

Exposed, its astronomical number
sings both day and night
at frequencies far above the human register

and rids the body
of poisonous spirits.
Many can be collected directly
into a killing jar or other container
without the use of a net.
Preserved, they will keep
indefinitely.

Habitat

It is impossible
to transplant time,

to dig up without injury
the full root system

bluish, delicate, forked,
neither male nor female.

Transverse candelabra
seen only with the aid
of a binocular microscope,

it spreads and speeds
faster than it dies.

Uncanny

The origin of adults
is shrouded in mystery.
Nothing is known
about what they first looked like
or the circumstances
that made their appearance possible.
Identification is complicated
by extreme variability;
nomenclature is incredibly jumbled;
species are juggled about
with capricious ease.
Many can change
their proportions
drastically, become
extremely contracted
or unnaturally distorted.
Sharply toothed, they may
be mistaken for ghosts,
but they break into pieces
at the slightest provocation,
so are best left alone.

Note: Comprised of words and phrases found in the National Audubon Society
field guide series and the Peterson field guide series

THE SLEEPERS

Weighted with chains, or hand-stitched into linen;
scrolled into satin coverlets like cocoons;
an inch above the cushions, lightly floating;
even from trees they sing, lashed to the branches—
bolt upright, arms extended, hair fanning out
like flame in all directions—

there is a creaking, there is a violent roaring—
turning, the grasses bend their heads;
in blazing streams the bees desert the hives
as clouds compress themselves to gather speed.

Oh the billowy beds of the world, the mats, the hammocks!
How can they endure this weight, the torrent
of the song to the bees, to the clouds, and to the grasses:

Birth is more terrible than death,
yet still shall we be born—and still rejoice!
But we beseech You, turn your eyes from us, Beloved,
for only Your gaze compels us to sing on.

DIFFICULT WORK

1.

When expunging a wave, you mustn't interfere
with the concavity between trough and crest,
or the suspended, churning furrows between peaks,
nor may you displace those intervals
where the luminous glass spheres
lining the wave's underbelly strike each other,
emitting the chime-tones required
for circular propulsion, the illusion
of forward movement, for it isn't water
that advances, but the disturbance itself
as it sculpts the surge, and then
abandons it to be lifted again.
Since a wave is almost nothing
but disappearance transposed as light,
you don't want to end up
with a scrunched or pleated surface—
we already have nearly a continent's worth
of shadows from all the smeary
attempts at erasure.

2.

The problem with trying to consume time
is that you can never get outside it,
and even if you did manage to slice
a serving's worth, you wouldn't eat it raw;
you'd need to roast or fry it,
but it's made up of varying consistencies,
some parts too sticky to burn,
others too frail to ignite.
Also, there are places where its flow
seems to self-reverse,

so that even if you *could* set it on fire,
the flames would meet each other
in mutual extinguishment.

More likely, after long effort,
you'd get only a sullen smoldering,
not the desired blaze.
And you can't even tell
whether you move *through* time,
parting it so that it closes up behind you,
or instead, occupy a bubble
that repels, bumps into,
or temporarily fuses with
your neighbors' bubbles.
Either way, to inhabit time
is to find yourself forever
ravenous in the middle.

3.

It's true that refreshment arises
from attention to the face,
and that you can't sketch your worst enemy
without falling a little in love.

The face is the freshest wound,
intersecting time
as a wave traverses space.

Identifiable primarily by its shyness,
the face suffers permanent arrival shock
just over the threshold between
nonexistence and being,

.

always permeable, nearly weightless,
flickering between sheerness and opacity,
lit by its own apprehension as it splits
the inner from the outer turbulence.

Nevertheless, every aficionado knows
that as well as the angel who troubles
the face's surface, and the after-angel
who smoothes it over again,

there's also the angel of the other side,
presiding over expressions that flow
in darkness behind the bone mask.

So when is it least impossible
to try to capture the face?

When it believes itself
to be unobserved;
when it's half-clad or all uncovered:
in weathers, passions, pains,
in children, sleepers, secret singers,
the dying and the dead.

But even then, the hand stammers
against its dimensional horizon,
and must start all over again,
straining to render what streams from
that luminous tissue, that corporeal frame.

4.

Attempting to recite from the transparent book
is like laboring to decode a swarm of bees,
the spaces between the words always
sinking and rising in agitated spirals.

The due date was so long ago,
you must be a library outlaw by now,
and a clumsy one, at that, because look,

the transparent book has fallen
open on the lawn, indistinguishable
from what it rests on—
grass, topsoil, substrate—
which it renders transparent, too.

Isn't it time to abandon your project
of reading to the dead?

Isn't it time to trust
that they can take in the story for themselves,
and disassemble its subtexts on their own?

SWIMMER

You must have been
daydreaming again,
losing speed,
for now you find yourself
lightly surrounded

by butter churns,
bushel barrels,
and a bevy
of wasp-waisted mannequins
with waxen heads
and green glass eyes,
all bobbing about you.

If you want to catch up
to the artifacts of your era,
you'll have to kick
that much harder.

WONDERS OF THE INVISIBLE WORLD

1.

Doesn't everybody get a strange life?
Don't we get to walk around
inside ourselves all day long,
and sleep there through the whole night?
Don't we have permanent access
to the magnum and the minimum opus,
the rising up and the sinking down?
Aren't we granted the right
to refrain from occupying
more than one place at a time,
from sharing the portable spaces we inhabit,
from being in the least interchangeable?
Doesn't it take all of our courage
to be *this* but not *that*,
no matter how incremental the distinctions
in this world where even the smallest entity
is epic to itself, and objects go precisely
to their own edges and then stop,
or at least hesitate?
Don't we all get the ocean
and the *idea* of ocean—
diffusion, resistance, and support—
along with those in-your-face heavens
of exponential blue,
cumuli performing their high-wire act
as the wind releases its flayed
and flaming exhalations?
And consecutive failures,
each more luminous than the last?
Don't we get to drink deeply
of the sun and grief and night
and other voluminous bodies?

And there's all this topiary profusion.
And there are things that are discrete,
things that overlap, things that can be
left to themselves, and things requiring
intermittent maintenance and repair.
There are things which once released
from their containers will never fit back in.
There are things we've torn apart
with our bare hands—
a few of them are even visible
here where it's been arranged for us
to be asynchronously lonely while
we tingle with the temporal heebie-jeebies,
as though preparing to lift off
with wings sutured together from
the mangled remains of defective feathers.
Up comes a small wind,
and the temperature begins to drop.
O bright wound of existence,
so feral and ferociously shy,
first wonder of the unseen world,
are you God, or just
some kind of emissary?
How chagrined we find ourselves
that we couldn't have made you up!—
nor water, whose work
is to taste like nothing,
nor air, whose work
is to look like nothing,
nor fire, whose work
is to billow in the bloodstream,
impersonating nothing
even as it burns.

2.

The second wonder is that certain spaces
are larger on the inside than on the outside.
To this the works of Heironymous Bosch attest
with excruciating lucidity.
Fortunately, there's nearly always an exit
or inversely, an entrance—
consider St. Anthony
whose desert was honeycombed
with caverns like a sponge.
He traced his own path backward,
arriving at an identical opening
on the opposite side of the mountain
he'd tunneled through all night.
Lifting his hands to the sun,
he saw that they were encrusted
with what might have been snow,
but resolved into tiny white shells
dropping from his stiff fingers
as he flexed them one by one.
Then it *was* the voice of the ocean
he'd heard in the darkness—
the voice, or the mountain's
memory of the voice.
That's when the fine mesh
of the net encompassing the heart
became the branching capillaries
of his own eyes,
and his tears found their way out
between the delicate knots,
for he had reached that place in the body
where salt flows out
from a point so infinitesimal
you can find it only
by diving through.

3.

The third wonder
is the boredom of children,
which can most accurately be compared
to a great linen tablecloth
borne in the beaks of four cranes
patiently circling the earth's skies,
seeking the one place
where they may lay it down.
They may never lay it down.
Thus, regarding the boredom of children,
there's nothing more to be said.

Interlude in the Manner of a Digression

Evaporation occurs on the threshold
between the visible and invisible.
Thus, it can be listed
but not assigned a number.
Evaporation means God spares us
a life weighed down by permanently
saturated towels and soggy dishcloths
beneath a scalding sky.

True, Noah learned fear
at the sight of those
heaped up, heaving tides,
but it wasn't till he beheld
the waves drawn back,
steam rising in columns
from the glistening soil
that he suffered his first
amazement.

4.

The fourth wonder is the act of falling.
If it were possible to map a fall,
we'd see that like reverse déjà vu,
it occurs in the mind
one iota of an instant
before it manifests in the body
as afterthought.
The mental fall is the bride;
the physical fall is the verger
sweeping up the rice.

5.

The fifth wonder is rumor and gossip,
third-hand testimony, a voice
navigating the turns
of a tale by intimate landmarks,
anecdotal evidence, snatches of narrative floating free
long after the speaker is forgotten.
The heiress, who hoping for a better man,
left her husband, and then a year later,
in remorse, gave him the fortune
he married someone else with.
And the graduate student who accepted the offer
of fifty-thousand dollars if he'd just take
this free ticket to Mexico, spend the night
in a hotel (*all expenses paid*!),
fly home the next day.
We salute people who speak
with ghosts and extraterrestrials;
we honor conversions, deconversions
not quite inaccessible in parallel time,

as though the little stories
are coalescing or the one big story is breaking down;
we trust how some almost-smothered part of us
imagines such reversals that even now
we can take ourselves by surprise.

6.

If the air is all happening at once,
it finds no need to hurry;
if it occurs in tiny spherules
it knows leisure
but no reason for delay.

Dissect a breath
to its smallest weather,
and you'll still have a saga,
flesh's first epiphany
whose inner lining
is stitched with flame.

Wave-like, it recedes and surges,
adoring all its habitations
with equal ardor in infinite exchange:
hello Attila, hello Jeanne d'Arc,
hello cat-sized horses galloping
through forests of gigantic primeval ferns—

breath transmuting into breath
in ecstasies of iteration

And into the future it bears us
like packs of sled dogs
through our sleep.

7.

Listen!
Holes are falling
through the universe,
passing through the sieve
for invisible things
which is itself invisible,
so we can never know
how fine the mesh is,
how tight the weave.

8.

Midwifing our arrivals
at their incorporeal city,
the dead are courteous
in that clinical way.
Here comes the next peak, they say,
Try to relax—knowing that we won't,
even though *won't* in the end
will spare us nothing.
Still, they don't chide,
remembering that we've had
no practice, that for each of us,
it's always the first time.

BLINK

Everyone was writing a dystopian novel,
and everyone had a podcast or at least a blog,
and every phrase that seemed like a good band name
turned out to be a band name already,
and the punishment for information
was more information, as was the reward,
and through almost an entire week,
real-time images of an actual black hole
scintillated around the globe
as we outsourced our disambiguation,
each of us gazing into a palmed incandescence
instead of the starry heavens above
or the reeking entrails of gutted sheep,
and every time we bought groceries
we re-titrated the amount of glysophates
we were willing to ingest,
but there were still pockets of local solace
scattered amidst the impending,
so it was possible to savor sushi
on the same day you declined to discard
an unfinished bottle of Tramadol—
how long would analgesics be available?—
and because we were ever more achingly cognizant
of the textured, fretted, speckled, tender underside of things,
art was either prophetic elegy or elegiac prophecy,
and for some of us, the projected time of collapse
corresponded to our own natural end,
though *Will I still be alive when the world is over?*
asked the nine-year-old as his mother marked
his birthday inches on the wall,
and in speaking of our situation there was social protocol

which consisted of reticence and restraint,
though sequence continued to coexist with simultaneity,
and the Lost and Found ceased not its overflow,
and newborns persevered in the struggle
to inhabit their own flailing,
and the young continued shining unaware,
and breath still wandered through our bodies
like a wickless flame,
everything unlikely and irreducible as always
in this dense serendipitous connotative world
clotted with decisions we hadn't noticed
until we found ourselves together on the other side,
and what was that just barely within our audible range,
the sound of events becoming retroactively inevitable,
or had we failed to notice
a single moment of no-taking-back,
when the nascent future flew out,
slick, new-hatched, through a chink, a crack,
a fissure, the proverbially yawning gap?
Now there we were moving swiftly,
no, suspended *inside* a momentum
whose shape we couldn't trace,
and all the algorithms were about
how we were more the same than different,
more different than the same,
and our pre-extinction consciousness
was just as inaccessible
as our pre-digital consciousness,
and any soul aspiring to reincarnate
would have to aim for someplace in the past—
how crowded it would be with multitudes

crammed into each of the much fewer
available human bodies back in the day!—
but were we, as a species, old or young?
Wasn't it only recently we'd all nestled
in the center of celestial crystalline spheres?
Now that which had been submerged was rising up,
and that which had stood high was going under,
and the little ice chapel in Helsinki
was thawing at the same rate it evaporated,
and the leafy places of the earth were limned with flame,
so why hadn't the teams been deployed
to peel away all the shadows, fold them tenderly
for cold storage lest they warp and scald?
Now the simplest of greetings meant,
Are we still here?
like children waking up through the night,
tiptoeing to the window to see if it's snowing.

ORDEAL

And now you must enter the forest of fiery hands.

You may not proceed in clusters or pairs—squeeze through the narrow gap alone, turn sideways, suck in your breath.

All the hands are ready to be plucked, ripe inside their flames.

Your strategy should be a combination of speed and aplomb—reach in boldly to extract a hand from its fibrous casing, and you won't be harmed, but if you hesitate, pausing to stroke the palm or test the fingers, you may find yourself singed.

Don't waste time attempting to locate identical hands; a degree of tactical incongruity may prove decisive in the endeavor to come. Particularly auspicious matches include a transparent hand with a polynomial hand, a shattered hand with a petrified hand, a mordant hand with a confectionary hand.

Understand that each hand you choose will immediately engulf your birth-hand, autografting to your wrist. Avert your gaze lest you spook it during this process, causing it to balk or bolt.

As soon as your selection is fully adhered, you must sing to it as it self-extinguishes. If you're the one who harvested the lone aqualuminous hand, understand that you'll be in immediate danger from the eleven assassins who have been seeking it without surcease through all the adjacent dimensions; report to us at once, and we'll issue the protective black diamond glove.

Once the cooling is complete, the forest will precipitously eject you. Should you try to force your way back in, you'll find the passage overgrown with brambles as though you'd never passed through.

Now you'll begin your march toward the sea together.

According to the mandate, you must press on in silence. You may exchange information only through expelling air currents by mouth in shapes appropriate to your meaning, a phenomenon that will suffer many names throughout the ages until it eventually comes to be known as whispering.

There will be seasons of snow and of bituminous winds, opaque cities you'll pass through like ghosts, and spectral cities shimmering around your density.

There will be the viscera of unidentifiable creatures strewn across the road; the sky as it basks and turns, drinking the luxuriant smoke of villagers ritually cremating the shadows of their dead; the terror that everything could at any moment become even one degree more beautiful.

By your third century, you'll be trudging as if in sleep, while inside the adoptive hands, which are also dozing, your birth-hands twitch and tremble like hunting dogs dreaming by the hearth.

All along the way, you'll sense the forest right behind you, pausing as you pause, breathing as you breathe, but looking back will be forbidden, so you'll never be able to determine whether this is actual pursuit or the hallucinatory after-effect of your sojourn there.

And all along the way, you'll anticipate waves and foam, the opening out of atmosphere into saturated distance.

But when you finally reach the shore, though these components will indeed be in place, the scene will feel like nothing you'd expected, because you yourself will have changed. Are you bulky or buoyant?

You'll long to linger, caressing the horizon with your gaze in the near-dusk plumy with incandescence as clouds pile up impossibly overhead.

Nevertheless, you must walk straight into the water while the sand sucks at your feet and you wonder if that crackling in your brain is your hair freezing to your scalp or the static of submerged constellations.

You'll step deeper, ever deeper.

Now you are traversing the very bottom of the world wherein hide treasures of darkness and of the night.

Now the bearer of the lone aqualuminous hand will remove their black diamond glove, finger by finger, lighting you to the spot where the mighty vessel sank so long ago.

There can be no exemptions. It will take every one of those hands to dredge up the hull and turn the great ship around.

ACKNOWLEDGMENTS

Work in this collection has appeared and/or is forthcoming, some pieces in previous forms or versions, in *The Alabama Literary Review* ("A Diagrammed Sentence," "Grip," "Habitat," and "Men as Trees, Walking"), *Bearing Myrrh* (a passage from "Wonders of the Invisible World"), *Bacopa Literary Review* ("Mystique Academy"), *Borfski Press* ("Three Little Disappointment Songs"), *Café Irreal* ("The Invisibility Cloak"), *Free State Review* 2018 Heavenly Creatures Contest winner ("Fathom"), *Gingerbread House Literary Magazine* ("Rising Time"), *How to Write a Form Poem* by T.S. Press ("Three Centos"), *Ice on a Hot Stove: Poems from the Converse Low Residency MFA Anthology*, Clemson University Press ("Blink" and "Mystique Academy"), *James Dickey Review* ("Outskirts" and "The Last Human Being Who's Not on Facebook"), *Jasper Writes!* ("Abundance," and "Losing Your Phone Is Worse than Losing Your Soul Because at Least if You Have Your Phone, You Can Text Your Soul"), *The Laurel Review* ("A Bedtime Story," "Three Centos," and "The Ordinary Course of Things"), *Los Angeles Review* ("Upkeep"), *MacQueen's Quinterly* ("Metaphorically Speaking," "The Perforating Spider," "Print," and "Weathers"), *Mudlark* ("A Bedtime Story," and "Pre-Headache"), *New Ohio Review* ("Grounded," "The New Loneliness," "The Virgin Mirror," and "Scatter,"), *Poetry WTF* ("Three Centos" and "The Ordinary Course of Things"), *Postcard Poems and Prose* ("Book Soup"), *Right Hand Pointing* ("Swimmer"), *Small House Pamphlet Series* ("Ordeal"), *Twyckenham Notes* ("The Deep Cross-Sectional Plunge," "Pencil Shop," and "Speak"), *Valparaiso Poetry Review* ("Blink"), *Vitamin ZZZ* ("A Bedtime Story" and "The Prisoners"), and *The Weekly Hubris* ("Rising Time," reprinted).

Big Thanks for editorial comments go out to Jon Bateman, Sarah Blackman, Wyn Cooper, John Gallaher, Mary Keneagy, Charlotte Matthews, Meg Pokrass, Jordan Rice, the members of the Ruminators Group, Veronica Schuder, and Susan Tekulve.

Photo by Jon Bateman

Claire Bateman is the author of eight other poetry books: *Scape* (New Issues Poetry & Prose, 2016), *Locals* (Serving House Books, 2012), *Coronology* (Etruscan Press, 2010), *Leap* (New Issues, 2005), *Clumsy* (New Issues Poetry & Prose, 2003), *Friction* (Eighth Mountain Poetry Prize, 1998), *At the Funeral of the Ether* (Ninety-Six Press, 1998), and *The Bicycle Slow Race* (Wesleyan University Press, 1991). Her fiction collection, *The Pillow Museum*, is forthcoming from FC2 in early 2025. She has been awarded Individual Artist Fellowships from the National Endowment for the Arts, the Tennessee Arts Commission, and the Surdna Foundation, as well as the New Millennium Writing Award (twice) and two Pushcart Prizes, and has taught at the Greenville Fine Arts Center, Clemson University and various workshops and conferences. She is also a visual artist.